William Knowler, Charles Harding Firth

Papers Relating to Thomas Wentworth

William Knowler, Charles Harding Firth

Papers Relating to Thomas Wentworth

ISBN/EAN: 9783337396930

Printed in Europe, USA, Canada, Australia, Japan

Cover: Foto ©ninafisch / pixelio.de

More available books at **www.hansebooks.com**

PAPERS

RELATING TO

THOMAS WENTWORTH,

FIRST EARL OF STRAFFORD.

FROM THE MSS. OF DR. WILLIAM KNOWLER.

EDITED BY

C. H. FIRTH, M.A.

PRINTED FOR THE CAMDEN SOCIETY.

M.DCCC.XC.

PREFACE.

THE papers hereafter printed are taken from the Manuscripts of Dr. William Knowler, editor of the two volumes of Strafford letters published in 1739.

On the death of William second Earl of Strafford in 1695 the title of Lord Raby passed to his cousin Thomas, grandson of William Wentworth younger brother of the first Earl of Strafford. This Thomas Lord Raby was created Earl of Strafford in 1711, and was one of the negotiators of the treaty of Utrecht. But the second Earl of Strafford had devised most of his estates, including Wentworth Woodhouse, to his nephew Thomas Watson, son of Edward second Lord Rockingham, and Anne daughter of the first Earl of Strafford. Thomas Watson Wentworth, son of this Thomas Watson, and therefore great grandson of the first Lord Strafford, was created successively Baron Malton (1728), Earl of Malton (1734), and Marquis of Rockingham (1746). He undertook the publication of a selection from his ancestors' papers. They were " selected," says the dedication which the editor addressed to his patron, " from a vast treasure of curious manuscripts by yourself, and published according to your Lordship's own directions and instructions, to vindicate his memory from those aspersions, which it is grown too fashionable to cast upon him, of acting upon arbitrary principles, and being a friend to the Roman Catholics."

Of Dr. William Knowler, the editor of the two volumes printed

in 1739, Nichols gives the following account: " William Knowler
was the third son of Gilbert Knowler, gent. of Stroud House at
Herne in Kent; baptised May 9, 1699. He was educated at St.
John's college Cambridge ; B.A. 1720 ; M.A. 1724 ; LL.D. Com.
Reg. 1728. He was chaplain to the first Marquis of Rockingham,
who presented him first to the rectory of Irthlingborough (commonly
called Artleburrow, between Wellingborough and Higham Ferrers),
and afterwards to the more valuable one of Boddington, both in
Northamptonshire. He died in December 1773." Dr. Knowler prepared for the press in 1766 a translation of Chrysostom's Commentary
on St. Paul's epistle to the Galatians, which was never published
(Nichols, Literary Anecdotes of the Eighteenth Century, vol. ii.,
p. 129; see also for further particulars, vol. viii., 401, and Illustra-
tions of Literature, iv. 427).

It is possible that in the editing of the Strafford letters Dr.
Knowler had some assistance from William Oldys. " From the year
1724 to 1730 Oldys resided in Yorkshire and spent most of his
time at the seat of the first Earl of Malton, with whom he had been
intimate in his youth. In 1729 he wrote an ' Essay on Epistolary
Writings, with respect to the Grand Collection of Thomas Earl of
Strafford, inscribed to the Lord Malton '" (Thoms, Memoir of
William Oldys, 1862, p. viii.). Mr. Thoms, following the lead of
Mr. Bolton Corney, suggests that this Essay may have been of some
service to Lord Malton and his chaplain in the selection of letters
for printing (Bolton Corney, Curiosities of Literature Illustrated,
p. 113). The Essay itself is probably still at Wentworth Woodhouse.

It remains now to give some account of the source of the papers
which follow. They are entirely derived from copies found amongst
Dr. Knowler's papers. In 1884 I purchased from Mr. George, the
well-known Bristol bookseller, a box of Dr. Knowler's papers,
which he had bought from the Rev. T. W. Openshaw, of Bristol

Grammar School, whose wife is descended from the editor of the Strafford papers.[a] The contents of the box were of a very miscellaneous nature. There were a number of Dr. Knowler's sermons, two imperfect copies of the Strafford letters in sheets, the manuscript from which that work was printed, and a number of miscellaneous notes made by the editor during its preparation.[b] There were also copies of several papers relating to Strafford, some of which are now printed. There was in addition a brief correspondence between Dr. Knowler and a certain Henry Goddard, which throws some light on the principles adopted by the former in editing the letters.

" SIR,

" I s[d] have made an earlier acknowledgment for y[e] civilities I rec[d] f[m] you at Wentworth but was desirous to send you at the same time a copy of y[e] odd remark made by Sir John Wentworth[c] upon y[t] celebrated lre of L[d] Straffords to King Charles to persuade him to give his assent to y[e] Bill of Attainder, w[ch] I mentiond to you w[n] you communicated y[r] design of publishing the whole collection & s[d] have sent you much sooner but have been confind by y[e] weather & did not get to Howsham till yesterday. The remark is

[a] Rev. John Knowler, LL.D. m. 1749, Mary Dalton.
    |
    Mary Knowler m. 1772, Edward Derby, of Boddick, Oxon.
    |
    Mary Derby m. 1806, Rev. John Hyde, Rector of St. Martin's,
    | [Oxford.
    Edward Hyde m. 1836, Rachel Early.
    |
    Anne Hyde m. Rev. T. W. Openshaw.

[b] Dr. Knowler's keys to the cyphers employed in Strafford's letters are now in the Bodleian Library.

[c] Sir John Wentworth, of North Elmsal, Yorkshire, was created a baronet July 28, 1692, and died April 25, 1720, aged 47. The family of Wentworth of North Elmsal was an early offshoot of the family of Wentworth Woodhouse, to which Strafford belonged (Hunter, *South Yorkshire*, ii. pp. 82, 451). The late Lord Strafford referred to is William, second Earl, who died in 1695 (Collins, ix. 410).

in S^{ir} John's hand as follows, *They say my late Ld Strafford hath ye original lre under his father's hand & y^t this was but to move pity, no desire to die.*

" As all the best Historians are clear in ye particular of Ld Straffords writing yt lre to the King one can't I think well doubt of ye truth of it, but in my opinion tis so farr fm being a good reason for the Kings passing the Bill y^t He is less excusable than if Ld Strafford had never wrote such a letter.

" In looking over Sir John Wentworth's papers for this remark I found copies of several lres wch by ye dates & subject matter of them must have been wrote by Ld Strafford wn Ld Deputy of Ireland, & in case they be not in y^r collection I will send you copies of them, I have taken down ye directions & a few lines at ye beginning of each lre by wch you will easily see whether they be copies of those you already have."

Mr. Goddard then gives a list of eight letters, copies of which were amongst Sir John Wentworth's papers.

" There are several more letters, but I imagine you have ye originals & shall therefore trouble you no more at present nor untill I have ye pleasure of hearing fm you wch I hope will be as soon as tis convenient & yt you will be so good to let me know if you have these lres, if not I shall copy them over at leisure & send em ye first opportunity.

" Y^r method of publishing the letters I think farr preferable to yt of subscription on many accounts, all who either are or wou'd be acquainted with english history will be desirous to have them so y^t you need not fear ye impression will lie long on yr hands; the arguments you have drawn up in defence of Ld Strafford's conduct in some particulars y^t are objected to him seem to me very just & clearly & strongly express'd, but if I may take ye liberty of giving you my opinion you have confined y^{r}self too much by bringing them into y^r dedication to Ld Malton, whose zeal for ye true inte[rest] of his Country, the worth of his private character, [and] well plac'd generosity as a Patron &c., will afford subject enough for y^t part of yr work & I think ought not to be passed by at a time wⁿ it must be own'd the moral taste is not very fashionable. Your defence also of Ld Straffords conduct might be somew^t enlarg'd, I imagine, by ye assistance of ye letters & you w^d probably meet with some circumstances in the historians of y^t remarkable period for yr purpose, I remember a passage in Dr. Welwood's memoirs, by wch it plainly appears yt his principal Accuser (& I suppose ye rest of ye party of wch Mr. Pym was a leader) had resolved to endeavour his ruine long before it was possible for him to give them any just grounds; this is ye passage in Welwood p. 45.[a] When the Earl, then Sir Thos Wentworth was upon making his peace with ye Court, he gave Mr. Pym some obscure intimation of it. Pym understanding his drift stopd him short with this expression, You need not use all this art to tell me y^t you have a mind to leave us: But remember w^t I tell you, you are going to be undone : & remember yt though you leave us now I will never leave you while yr head is upon yr shoulders. I shall not trouble you with any other apology for ye freedom I have us'd with you on this occasion except yt of ye obligation I thought myself under to give you my opinion with sincerity wch is too often an excuse for impertinence in others as well as, Sir,

" Yr oblig'd hmble servt

" HENRY GODDARD.

" P.S. The length and dullness of my lre may I fancy have prepard you to relish ye following piece of wit:

" A receipt to preserve a Man

" Set him in ye Sunshine of a Court till his Volatile Spirits are evaporated, take his Reason and place it under a Shade till it is perfectly cool. Consult y^r Herbal to find in a proper soil an armfull of ye following Spring-flowers, Youth, Beauty & cheerfulness, then take two Summer Plants Economy & Serenity & mix these well together with an equal quantity of self denyal & discretion; when y^r man is fitly prepard add these ingredients to him & set him

[a] Memoirs of the most material transactions in England for the last hundred year preceding the Revolution in 1688, by James Welwood, M.D. 1700, p. 48.

in a quiet place till they are all incorporated together & you will find He is compleatly Preserved.

" N.B. This is a Sweetmeat delicate to ye eye but exquisite to ye Taste. Confectioners often miscarry by putting sower & bitter into ye composition, the best rec^t is at Marston in ye good Ladys own keeping & the sweetest flowers for ye use are thought to grow at Oswaldkirk. [This was pinnd into the Lady's rec^t-book by her husband].

" Direct to me at Foston near York, to be left at Mr. Stainton's on ouse-bridge in York.

> " To
> " The Revd. Dr. Knoller
> at the Right Honble the Earl of
> Malton's at Wentworth House,
> near Rotherham,
> Yorkshire."

Dr. Knowler replied to Mr. Goddard in the following letter, of which a rather illegible draft is preserved amongst his papers.

" SIR,

" I am much obliged to you for your kind Letter, and the trouble you so generously offer to undertake to complete the Collection of my Lord Strafforde's Letters. Those that you have are undoubtedly his, but four or five of them are imperfect, & want a complementary Introduction of four or five lines. I could wish you would look into y^t from Sr Arthur Hopton, Nov. 24, 1638, about ye middle you will find this Passage, *I must not neglect to tell your Lordship, that I find very good Inclinations brought hither from* 308 *concerning* 411. Who 308 is I am uncertain, perhaps you may have it in words, 411 is the Prince Palatine outed at the time of his Patrimony. My Lord Strafforde's Reply to this in your Copy is imperfect, it begins with a Passage concerning Tyrconel, an Irish Rebell & Fugitive, and in speaking of him is used some Cypher, which I am forced to turn into Asteriscs, not knowing how to read it. I shall be obliged to you for a Copy of 2 of my Ld Str. Letters—

" Feb. 10, 1638, to Cottington, and
" Feb. 28, 1638, to Ld Admiral.

" These I never saw, tho' they are to two favourites, whom his Lordship would be open to, & they fall in a critical time, which makes me more inquisitive & desirous to see them. I shall not trouble you for any more, because it is not intended to publish every Letter, but the Principal ones; there is four or five times the number of Letters uncopied for one transcribed, & yet I believe those that shall glean them over again wont find many things material omitted.

" Historians give a Letter of ye 4th of May to the King^a & give very different Reasons for it, some . . . . . others strong desire to settle ye Peace of ye Kingdom, as the letter itself bears, Sir John Wentworth, art; where Sr John Wentworth learnt my Lord Strafforde ye son had it, I know not, but neither my Lord nor his Father ever saw it.

" The first Reason depends upon ye credit of Sr Wm Balfour, the second is contradicted by his dying Speech, where he begs the Audience to consider, w^r the beginning of a Reformation sh^d be written in blood, that he thinks they are in a wrong way: and the 3^d He was not capable of. Indeed the whole is contradicted by y^t ejaculation of his upon the Bill's being past, Put not your trust in Princes, hinting at ye story's solemn Promise, that he should not suffer in Life, Honour or Estate. However be it as it will I have no thoughts of entring into disquisitions of this nature, my business being solely to copy and print faithfully, & then leave the world to

---

ª The authenticity of the letter is attacked by Carte, Life of Ormond, ed. 1851, vol. i. pp. 275-278. He affirms it to be a forgery, and quotes a report that the second Earl of Strafford used to say that his father told him, on the night before his death, that " he had never wrote any such letter, and that it was a mere forgery of his enemies, in order to misguide the King to consent to his death." But the evidence of Sir George Radcliffe is conclusive proof of its genuineness. See Gardiner, History of England, ix. 361, where the question is discussed.

judge from these Letters wrote when the things were in agitation long before any Impeachment was thought of or feared. Whether his Lordship had these traiterous Intentions in every act he did which the Articles charge him with. This point 'tis true is already cleard up in his Answers upon Trial in Rushworth's Collection, but that is so long as I fear few have patience to read it, otherwise I think it would give them full satisfaction. But I must have done & not tresspass too far upon your good nature. I have no such Receipts to send back you gave me, & but little News, perhaps it may not be disagreeable to Lady W. to know, Mr. Wellbye & his Lady are expected in a few days at Rewerfield, they have left Scotland above a week, but this 'tis probable is no News to her Ladyship. Pray make my Compliments at Housham, and return my thanks for this favour, as I heartily do to yourself & am

" Your obliged humble Servt,

" W. KNOW[LER].

" Wentworth House,
   " Oct. 22ᵈ, 1737."

In a second letter which is not now in existence, Mr. Goddard sent copies of the two letters to Cottington and Northumberland, as desired by Dr. Knowler. They are printed on pp. 7, 8. He also added a list of several others which were amongst Sir John Wentworth's papers.[a]

[a] As the originals are at present inaccessible, a list of those letters which are not in the printed collection is subjoined :—

(1). The Lord Deputy to the Lord Keeper upon his requesting that Lord Holland might be examined as a witness in the Star Chamber case betwixt him and Sir Piers Crosby, dated Dublin, Dec. 10, 1638.

(2). To the Lord Keeper, 16 April, 1639, on the same subject.

(3). To the Lord Admiral, April 15, 1639.

(4). To Lord Cottington, April 16, 1639.

(5). To Sir Henry Vane, Dublin, April 29, 1639.

(6). To Sir Henry Vane, Dublin, 14 May, 1639.

(7). 24th May, Strafford to ——— (no address).

(8). To the Lord Admiral, 26 May, 1639, Dublin.

(9). To Sir H. Vane, Dublin, 30 May, 1639.

Dr. Knowler acknowledged the copies and enclosures in the following letter :—

" DEAR SIR,

" I return you now not only my own, but what is much more valuable, my Lord Malton's thanks for ye trouble you have taken about ye E. of Str. Letters. I drew out a List of those not transcribed & presented it to his Lordship, who upon consulting his books over again found every one of them, & told me, He had passed over them by design, & did not think them proper to be made publick at present. Indeed there was y^t care taken by my Ld Str. himself in having his Letters entered into Books, y^t I am now persuaded there are none but w^t my Lord Malton has, and those which have been copied by some particular friends have not been copied entirely, but ye principal parts only, as these of Sr John's appear to be by ye beginnings of them. the Letter you sent of 28 feb. 38 to ye Ld Adm. has some pretty flowers in it, yet ye matter is much ye same wth y^t of ye 10 of the same month & year. How ye Q. was instrumental to Strafforde's Death I am not able to say,[a] but this I know that there was no love lost between them. He c^d not be at her superstitious worship, & had disobliged her in not suffering the Papists to resort to St Patrick's Well in Ireland for miraculous cures, & I am persuaded all of that party rejoiced at his Death. I know not yet on w^t footing they will be published, can't guess at the Price of a Copy, nor ye Number, but be they more or less I doubt not but to be able to procure any number for your friends, & I believe they won't think their money ill laid out. I am entirely against Subscriptions, so that there will be no need of any application till it be near finished, & then ye quicker they are called for, the better certainly for me, & I will make bold to trouble you with a Letter when y^t time comes. On Wednesday morning

---

[a] The notion that the Queen was instrumental to Strafford's death is founded on the mistaken belief that she was his enemy; any hostility to Strafford on her part had ceased to exist long before his trial. See Gardiner, History of England, ix. 366.

Lady M. was safely delivered of a d. The day is highly honoured by the birth of the Princess Louisa the dutchess of Cleveland & now of ye Lady H. W. I made your compliments to Mr. Wellby. He intends for London after Xstmas & I hear has some hopes of sitting.

"I am, Dr Sir, your obliged humble serv^t,

"Wm K."

PAPERS RELATING TO THOMAS WENTWORTH, FIRST EARL OF STRAFFORD.

I.

Sr Thomas Wentworth, Bar^t, to Sr Robert Askwith, K^t.

SIR,

Having been enjoined by some of my nearest friends to stand at this Election for Knight for the Parliament with Sr George Calvert his Majesty's Principal Secretary, and having now declared ourselves, are to try the affection of our friends, among which number I have of long esteemed yourself to be unto me well assured. I must therefore hereby move you very effectually, earnestly to sollicite all your neighbours and friends that you have interest in, in York, to give their voices with us at this next choice, which is to be made, upon Christmas day, which your kind and respectfull endeavours, as I shall ever be mindfull to requite, as an argument of your true affection towards me, and in the nature of an especiall curtesy, so will I undertake, when I come at London (for I know we shall have you a Member of the House) to carry you to Mr. Secretary, make you known to him, not procure you only many Thanks from him, but that you shall hereafter find a readiness and cheerfulness to do you such good Offices as shall lie in his way hereafter. Lastly, I hope to have your Company with me at Dinner that day, where you shall be most welcome. And so desiring answer, I remain your very assured and affectionate friend,

TH. WENTWORTH.*

Wentworth Woodhouse,
Dec. 7, 1620.

* See Strafford Letters, i. 11, where this letter was originally to have been printed. On second thoughts Dr. Knowler, or possibly Lord Malton, decided to omit it.

II.

The Lord Mohun to the Lord Deputy.

MY MOST HONOURED LORD,

˙Your great and weighty cause received two days; the first in proofs, the second in censure. Your envious and ingrate enemy (as may they all be) is utterly confounded. Your Honour is advanced and sett off to that politick advantage as the mouths of the clamorous are stopped, and the hearts of your hidden Enemies are convicted, as conscious of your Integrity and Honour. The Court had a full Presence both days, though, unfortunately, my Lord Cottington's sickness held him thence. Relations of particulars are so exactly given your Lordship by others as (though I have quoted all) I spare them as things which I fear would be impertinent and troublesome.

Some observations of discernings between man and man in passage of the censure shall in due time be rendred by your servant. Let envy now mutter, she dare not talk. It was a brave chosen cause, and directed by God for future ends of his own glory in you.

I have also dived into the heads of the ablest Irish here, with whom I have had good Relation since my Lord Chichester's time, in accusation of whom they were then imployed. And, I protest, my Lord, for ought I can discern, they all contribute their generall affections to your Lordship's praise and honour, and vow they have not greater hope in the Gods' than in your Wisdom and Worth, for the Reduction of that Country from Barbarism to Civility.

My Lord, your servant is now settled with his family in London expecting your Commands, wherein he may do service, for otherwise he will assume the modesty to be spare in writing, knowing how flat a thing Complement is, to a man of your Fire and Nature. That Modesty shall shorten these sudden lines, whose closure must give your Lordship this assurance (that for ought your servant can yet discern, for my Lord is not yet in London), the house of Clare

stands affected as it was, which I beseech your Lordship believingly
to receive from the assured Faith and Duty of

Your Lordships

Most humble Servant,

J. OKEHAMPTON.[a]

Nov^{bris} ult°, 1633.

III.

[This letter marks one of the stages of the quarrel between Strafford
and Richard Boyle, Earl of Cork. Cork was cited before the
Castle Chamber for illegally possessing himself of Church lands—
the lands belonging to the College of Youghal being specified. The
progress of the case is noted in Strafford's Letters (vol. i. pp. 305,
347, 379, 449). A detailed history of it is given in the diary of the
Earl of Cork recently printed by Dr. Grosart ·(Lismore Papers,
Series I, vol. iv. pp. 46, 53, 59, 61, 68, 83, 106, 113-118). Finding himself in danger of a heavy sentence, Cork sought to obtain
leave to come over to England, and submit himself and his cause to
the King (ibid. pp. 117, 125). On Oct. 20, 1635, his messenger
returned with letters in his favour, including that from Windebanke
which is now printed. The letters, says Cork, "signified his
Majesty's pleasure that when all examinations in the Starr Chamber
sute were taken and published, and that the Lord Deputy had
certefied the state of the cawse and his opynon therof, that then I

---

[a] John Mohun of Boconnock, Cornwall, was created Lord Mohun of Okehampton,
co. Devon, 15 April, 1628, and died in 1644 (Dugdale Baronage, p. 461). See
Forster's Life of Sir John Eliot, passim. The cause mentioned is the suit between
Wentworth and Sir David Foulis. See Rushworth, ii. 215; Strafford Letters, i. 145, 167.

should be licensed to carry them over and present them to his Majesty, and submitt myself to his own censure. I delivered those two letters to the Lord Deputy, who was veary muche offended with me for procuring them, as if I had appealed from his justice, and from the power and integretie of this State, affirming he would wryte to answer his Majesty and alter that direction if he could and would receav a new command from the King er he would obey this; we discoursed privately in his gallery three howres at the least and in conclusion he promised me to forbear doing or writing anything till his certeficate was prepared till after examination and publication" (*ibid.* p. 130). Strafford however had before this, on 26 August, 1635, written to Laud arguing very strongly in anticipation against the course of action ordered in Windebank's letter (Strafford Letters, i. 459). He now wrote a brief letter to the King, pointing out that the directions given in Windebank's letter were directly contrary to those given him in a letter of Oct. 4, from Laud, and asking which he was to follow (*ibid.* p. 477). He succeeded apparently in obtaining power to proceed with the case, or to stay further proceedings as he thought fit. The Earl of Cork was eventually obliged to pay a fine of £15,000, to avoid public disgrace and a heavier sentence. " I prayed him to consider well," says Cork, " whether in justice he could impose so great a fyne upon me. Whereunto he replyed, Gods wounds, sir. When the last Parliament in England brake upp, you lent the King fifteen thousand pounds. And afterward in a very uncivill unmannerly manner you pressed his Majestie to repay it you. Whereupon I resolved, before I came out of England to fetch it back againe from you, by one meanes or other. And now I have gotten what I desired, you and I wilbe frends hereafter" (Lismore Papers, Series II. iii. 257).]

Mr. Secretary Windebank to the Lord Deputy.[a]

MY LORD,

His Majesty hath been pleased to command me to acquaint your
Lordship with a proposition lately made to him by the Lord
Chamberlain and the Earl of Salisbury in favour of the Earl of
Corke; who having offered to submit the business, for which he is
now questioned, entirely to his Majesty, and to make such acknow-
ledgements of his offence, and pay such sums of money by way of
Pecuniary Mulct, and to restore to the Church such lands and
possessions as he is charged to leave unduely gotten from it, as his
Majesty shall think fit, when the cause shall be certified by your
Lordship. And lastly, that this shall be done with such reservations
of Respect and Honour as are due to your Person, and to the
Place you hold under his Majesty there, humbly imploring your
favour and concurrence herein. Their Lordships have hereupon
been humble Suitors to his Majesty to take these Offers into his
Princely Consideration, and to remitt only that part of the publick
censure, which carries with it not only a present but a future note
and stain to remain upon Record to Posterity upon him and his
house. His Majesty therefore, well weighing these Offers, and in
his goodness liking well this dutifull Submission, which deserves
some mitigation, especially in a person of his quality now in the
declination of his years, and that heretofore had so eminent a part
in the government of that Kingdom, and finding them not altogether
disproportionable to his offence as it now stands charged, hath
commanded me to signify his pleasure to your Lordship, that
immediately upon Publication had in this cause, you make certificate
thereof, and of the true State of this Business to his Majesty, and
that you forbear to proceed to an hearing untill you shall have
demanded of him, whether he will fully and freely submitt to his

---

[a] The Strafford Letters contain the Lord Deputy's answer to this letter, which is
addressed to the King (i. 477; see also pp. 449, 459, 479).

Majesty or not ; which if he do, then you are to suffer the said Earl of Corke (otherwise not, but to proceed against him according to Law) to repair hither immediately into England (any former signification of his Majesty's Pleasure to the contrary notwithstanding) to give his personal attendance upon his Majesty, that so his Majesty may receive from himself such submissions and satisfactions as shall be thought fit. In the meantime, his Majesty expects that together with that Certificate your Lordship shall send your advice, what Sum of Money, and what other satisfaction it is fit he should give both to his Majesty and to the Church, together with whatsoever else your Lordship shall find most conducing to his Majesty's Honour and Advantage. His Majesty is pleased to yield thus far at the Intercession of the Lord Chamberlain and the Earl of Salisbury, who desire nothing but to preserve this nobleman, now so nearly allied to their family, from publick disgrace; which his Majesty holds not unreasonable upon the motives and grounds before represented.

This being all I have in charge from his Majesty at this time, I present my humble service to your Lordship and rest

Your Lordship's
Most humble & faithfull servant,
FRAN: WINDEBANK.

Westminster.
Oct. 22, 1635.

IV.

The Lord Deputy to my Lord Cottington, dated Dublin, Feb. 10, 1638.[a]

I am extremely overjoyed to understand of the greate forwardness expressed in England towards his Majesty on this great occasion, and his Majesty's so speedy advancing to Yorke will give a greate

---

[a] Copied by Goddard from Sir John Wentworth's papers and sent to Dr. Knowler; see preface, p. ix.

countenance to the cause itself; all here are for peace, and the Scots amongst us very quiet, but, however, wee will bee watchfull over them. Our standing army of 3,000 horse and foote are in good condition ; I shall have by Whitsontide eight thousand spare armes, twelve field pieces, and eight great ordinance ; I am commanded to quicken my Lord of Antrim to have his forces in readiness, but I protest I neither know nor can I learne of any he hath, I knowing that this terme an extent goes against all his lands for three hundred pounds. It's appointed mee to furnish him with armes but were it not best think you to keepe them for ourselves, at least unless we know how to be paid for them, etc.,

WENTWORTH.

---

v.

The Lord Deputy to the Lord Admiral, dated Dublin, 28th of February, 163⅞.[a]

The use that's made of my absense I feele most sufficiently, and

---

[a] This letter was sent by Henry Goddard to Dr. Knowler ; see preface, pp. vi., ix. The list of letters which he gives includes several to Vane and Northumberland, printed in vol. ii. of the Strafford Papers.

Lord Holland had for some time been hostile to Wentworth, and had carried stories against him to the King (Strafford Letters, ii. 125, 189). He objected to be examined as a witness in Wentworth's case against Sir Piers Crosby in the Star Chamber, and pleaded his privilege as a Privy-councillor (*ibid.*, 230, 277). Though he was finally compelled by the King's command to give evidence, it does not appear to have been of much value (p. 307). See the reports of Crosby's case, Rushworth, vol. iii. 888-900, Cal. State Papers, Dom. 1639. Wentworth had also just received from the Earl of Northumberland, then Lord Admiral, the news that, thanks to the influence of the Queen and the Marquis of Hamilton, Holland had been made General of the Horse, for the northern expedition, in place of Essex (Strafford Letters, ii. 276). With reference to Wilmot, an old opponent of the Lord Deputy, the latter observes in a letter to Northumberland, " The endeavoures I bear to bring in my Lord Wilmot and some are pleased to affect it the rather, as that which would much displease me " (*ibid.*, p. 280).

in consideration of it had once obtained leave to come over this spring; but since his Majesty hath ordered my stay, which I shall readily submit to. The question betwixt my Lord Holland and me touching his examination by him avoided by mee pressed is not so much whether I shall have any advantage by it as whether I shall have it at all or noe, so as to my understanding I have granted as much as I coveted, although not in so full a manner as I ought to have had it, and yet why his Lordship should boast so much of his gains good faith I see not, onely little things pleaseth some folks, and I am willing it should be so providing I suffer not by it. The cause were very barren out of which that noble gentleman could not fetch something to magnifie himselfe by, and a happyness perchance it's to some natures that can delight and entertain themselves with small things, with these nowe and then a gathering of cockle shells on the Germain Coaste is a conquest of Britain; but his Lordship is able to do yet more, can gather glory to himselfe by making my Lord Wilmot Governour of Newcastle, nay that he had many yeares since obtained of his Majesty the making my Lord Wilmot a Barron of England, his Lordship may go on, as Sir R. Swift said to a gentleman that had extremely wearied all the company with a most tedious and impertinent discourse, but for all that his Lordship shall be examined, and find it a very hard matter to slip from under my fingers, but I shall advantage my cause as much by the setting forth his priviledge as a Councillor to the concealing of a truth as if he had ingeniously and nobly expressed it.

It troubles me to find your Lordship no better satisfied as to the councells and purposes now a foote for the defence of his Majesty and these Kingdoms; those great armies we speake of will I believe leave most men to seeke where the money can be raised that must defray them, for this not well foreseene aud provided for, to bringe so greate a number together & leave them for the necessitys of life to plunder our own country were a remedy worse than the disease, & no meanes as yet being settled in that important point mouves me to be of opinion his Majesty is of beliefe that by the name of those greate armies and some other private intelligencies he hath there is yet (in the King)[a] some hopes of allaying the storme and quieting the watters, wherein I beseeche God he may not find himselfe mightily mistaken, and so indeed dangerously mistaken, and that his Majesty's greate secresie turn not in a business of so many peeces mightily to the prejudice of his affaires; for he must be a fortunate servant indeed as well as wise that untaught, unguided by his Master's word and directions, can be able to serve according to the mind and liking of his superiors; it would be well for our greate chiefs that whilest they speake of these powerfull armies they would not scorn to take care of lesser matters which may bee effected, especially the securing of Carlisle and Berwick; good my Lord, press the King home in it especially to secure Berwick; it's reported four thousand are to be put into Newcastle, what I beseech your Lordship is your opinion if brought together under that pretence they seize upon Barwick, which they may march day and night too having their vituals carried by sea; certainly this would be a greate security to the English and a greate reputation to his Majesty's prudence and conduct: the bringing in the Earl of Holland was a strain of power God knows to little purpose considering that I do not take him to be so learned a Doctor in the Art as shoud render him worthy to be contended for to the discontentment of those who were placed before and every way as deeply skilled in the practise and profession as himselfe; but now it's done if I may speake it without offence to his Lordship's imaginary plenipotence, I am most confident it's more done than Holland's power was able to do for himself alone, and that he owes the glory of it cheefly to the Marquess[b]—it's not my opinion without grounds that the Marquess reserves some private expedient communicable only with the King, whereby he feedes perchance the passion that most

[a] Note by Mr. Goddard:

"N.B. The words above *in the King*, tho' writ exactly as I have transcribed them, in the copy, I look upon as a wise remark of Sir John Wentworth's by way of explanation."

[b] *i.e.* the Marquis of Hamilton.

reigns in us with a beliefe to wind up all in conclusion with peace; so long as he keeps all in that temper, he is sure to have a full measure of grace and trust; but when wee shall to our costs feele ourselves disappointed of that expectation, and by that means be cast fearfully behinde in the way to our preservation (which on my faith I believe will prove true), then perchance we may give our eyes the liberty to look about them, and shall plainly discern that ourselves which we will not allow any other so much as to point at, etc.

WENTWORTH.

VI.

A perfect account of the days and times of the Earl of Strafforde's first and second Journeys from Ireland into England; as also of his Lordship's Journey from London to the North, and so back to London, as followeth:—

My Lord's first Journey from Ireland, Sept. 1639. [By Mr. Littell].

Upon thursday ye 12th of September, 1639, his Lordship came from Dublin, took Ship, and landed upon friday ye 13th; that night to Chester.

Saturday the 14th to Cholmondley.

Sunday the 15th to Stone.

Monday the 16th to Litchfield.

Tuesday the 17th to Coventry.

Wednesday ye 18th to Daventry.

Thursday the 19th to Stony Stratford.

Friday the 20th to St Albans.

Saturday the 21st to London to his Lordship's House in Covent Garden.

My Lord's Journey from London to Ireland, Mar. 1639.

His Lordship remained at London until thursday the 5th of Mar. 1639, on which day his Lordship began his Journey towards Ireland, and in three laid Coaches came ye s^d 5th of March to Stony Stratford.

Friday the 6th of March to Daventry.

Saturday the 7th to Coventry.

Sunday ye 8th after Sermon and Dinner to Litchfield.

Monday ye 9th to Stone.

Tuesday the 10th to Chester.

Wednesday ye 11th to Hollywell.

Thursday ye 12th to Conway.

Friday ye 13th to Place Newith in Wales. Sr Art. Tirringham's.

Saturday the 14th ibidem.

Sunday 15th ibidem.

Monday the 16th to Lea.

Tuesday ye 17th at Lea.

Wednesday the 18th to Dublin, and there his Lordship staid untill Good Friday the 3^d of Apr. 1640.

My Lord's 2^d Journey from Ireland, Apr. 1640.

Upon friday the 3^d of April 1640, his Lordship came from Dublin, took Ship, and landed upon the day following, being Easter Eve the 4th; about 12 o'clock at night his Lordship came sick to Chester, and there continued sick at the Bishop's house all the week following, untill Saturday the 11th, and y^t night in a Litter to Mr. Wilbraham's house at Namptwich.

Sunday the 12th of April in Sr Thomas Delves his Litter to Stone, and so all the way to Lond. in ye same Litter.

Monday the 13th to Litchfield.

Tuesday the 14th to Coventry.

Wednesday the 15th to Daventry.

Thursday the 16th to Stony Stratford.

Friday ye 17th to St. Albans.

Saturday ye 18th to London, to my Lord of Leicester's House, where his Lordship remained from the saidth 18 of April until Monday the 24th of August following, and the most part of that time very dangerously sick.

My Lord's Journey to the North, Aug. 1640.

Monday ye 24th of Aug. in laid Coaches to Huntingdon.

Tuesday ye 25th to Newark.

Wednesday ye 26th to York.

Thursday 27th ibid.

Fryday ye 28th towards night his Lordship being sickly to Topcliffe.

Saturday ye 29th to Darington.

Sunday ibid.

Monday ye 31st back to North Allerton wth ye Army.

Tuesday ye 1st of Sept. to Topcliffe.

Wednesday the 2^d to Tollerton.

Thursday the 3^d to York.

And back to London, Nov. 1640.

His Lordship continued at York from the said third of September until Monday the 2^d of Nov. that night late to his Lordship's House at Wentworth Woodhouse.

Tuesday the 3^d, Wednesday ye 4th, and Thursday ye 5th ibidem.

Fryday ye 6th at Newark.

Saturday ye 7th at Stamford.

Sunday ye 8th at Huntingdon.

Monday ye 9th of Nov. his Lordship came of Horseback to Royston, and in two laid Coaches from thence to London.

VII.

[The John Cooke who addressed the following letter to Strafford
was the man who afterwards as solicitor for the Commonwealth
conducted the case for the prosecution during the trial of Charles I.
A royalist newspaper, Mercurius Elenticus No. 56, published in
1649 a somewhat scandalous sketch of Cooke's early life. After
describing him as leaving England for Ireland from reasons very
much to his discredit, it continues " Now in Ireland we have him
strutting in his plush and velvet, cringing for acquaintance and
screwing into the favour of the Earl of Strafford, who at length
took notice of his fair deportment, and saw something in him that
might deserve his countenance, but all this while knew none of his
qualities; nevertheless the statutes at large being then to be printed
the Lord Deputy commits the care thereof to this Cooke, whom he
appoints to revise the same and see they were faire and truly
printed.   And deposited a large summe of moneys in his hands to
defray the charge of printing.   But this worshipful gentleman
instead of correcting the prooves proves the second time a publique
trecherous knave, for he run into Italy with the money, where he
became a papist."   For the mere fact of the identity of the Cooke
employed in Ireland with the solicitor for the Commonwealth this
evidence seems sufficient.   The references to Geneva, and other
places where the regicide is known to have been during his travels,
serve to complete the proof.]

Mr. Cooke to the Lord Lieutenant of Ireland.

RIGHT HONOURABLE,
    I owe your Lordship more than I am worth for the gracious
aspect vouchsafed me in Ireland, where had I not been wanting to
myself I might have passed that time in a comfortable practise,

which has been spent in a disconsolate Pilgrimage. However, no man honours you more than myself, who do as cordially pray for your Lordship's Happiness as ever I did for my own Recovery, and not knowing how better to express my humble Duty than by presenting my humble mite (which is but as the pissing of a Wren to the Sea of your learned Counsell's Experience) I presume, in the lowest Degree of Humility that dutifull observance can imagine, to beseech your Honour not to disdain these few abrupt considerations proceeding ·from an heart fraught with Zeal to do you service, *Quod si fenestratum foret, cerneret Dominatio vestra hanc fixam, haud fictam fidem.* Your Lordship though now confined, yet I hope like Gold refined your Integrity by this Trial will be more conspicuous.

We young Lawyers conceive, that the Article, which most intrenches upon your Lordship is for supplanting and subverting Municipal Laws, and attempting to reduce all in the nature of a Lex Regia, which only the absolute Power of a Parliament can do. I lived in Ireland almost two years, and, *si ex pede Herculem,* I believe your noble Soul is not guilty of any one such single Cogitation. I have known many that have felt the reviving Heat of your Lordship's speedy Justice, whose very Entrails now bless you; and if upon lamentable Petitions, that poor Suitors were not able to contest with the great ones in a circular course of Justice, your Lordship have justly relieved them (that Tantalus like have spent many years in other Courts) in a speedy way of Justice, certainly this is not *supplantatio* but *plantatio,* not *subversio* but *supportatio Legis,* for *bis dat qui cito dat*: Delay of Justice being a kind of Denial of Justice, it being speedy Justice, which like speedy Remedies, cure the consumption of State. Your Lordship always observed, *Quod dubites ne feceris,* never making any Order till clearly resolved by the Reverend Judges, neither did your Lordship take cognizance of any causes but such as had been long depending in Courts of Justice, or those that concerned the Church, whereof there was great necessity, for that I have known Juries to go strangely against

the Evidence in those matters. But *dato non concesso*, 'tis clear
that such an article is no Treason within the Statute of 25 E. 3, 4,
as being rather an advancement than a depression of the King's
Honour. For, if a Judge shall deny the View and Essoigns and
other Legal Advantages this cannot be Treason, for, if the Common
Pleas should hold Plea of Murder, it would be a nullity, but no dis-
loyalty. And if that statute be only declaratory, yet there is a
clause, that if any doubtfull case arise, the Determination thereof is
referred to the next Parliament. For, no penal Statute is to be
extended, the reason whereof is rendered in that famous arraignment
of Sr Nicholas Throckmorton recorded by Hollinshead in the Life
of Queen Mary, that considering the private affection of the Judges
in that they were men, and subject to Error, it would be dangerous
to the subject to referr the extending construction of penal Statutes
to them, which might either through Fear of higher Powers be
seduced, or by ignorance and folly abused. Which report containing
much excellent learning about Treason is well worth your Lordship's
second Reading. It was doubted upon that Statute of 25, whether
to go about to deprive the King were Treason, because the words
are, imagine the Death of the King, without which Intention there
might be a Deprivation, and thereupon Statutes were made Temp.
Hen. 8 & E. 6 to that purpose, as the Book is in Bē Treason 24.
And the putting of an old Seal to a new Patent is not Treason, with
many other cases That the Judgment in Treason being so
ponderous, the Judges are not to extend any Laws beyond the
genuine Interpretation, and if any one had gone about to deprive
before those Statutes, although the next Parliament had made it
Treason, yet such a party would not have been guilty, because
penal Laws are never retrospective, and a man may not regularly
be attainted by Relation. *Mutare formulas Legis non est Proditio*,
saith Bartolus, *quia non sunt de Essentia Legis*, for *suum cuique
tribuere* is the principal, and the several forms of proceeding are but
as the Cabinet to preserve the Jewell. All Justice is originally in
the crown, and his Majesty constitutes his Judges, *ut Labor ei esset*

levior, and it is requisite, that every Magistrate should keep his own Jurisdiction, but if one *pro zelo Justitiæ* should encroach, this can be no traiterous Intention, for to make Justice pass with an easy charge, that those brambles of needless expence that grow about it might be rooted out, must needs be most beneficial to the Subject. Amulio Secretary to Grand Cosmio was accused *quod proditoriè Leges antiquas Etruriæ violasset, qui respondet illum celeriorem exequi Justiciam omissis Juris quisquilliis, cui concordatum est formulas Juris non esse ipsum Jus,* and expedite Justice can no more be called Treason, than Mithridate may be called Poyson.

That your Lordship should assume regal Power is very generally reported, but presumptive answer may stand for presumptive objection. 'Tis true you were Lord Deputy not Assignee of Ireland, nothing in your own Right, but *loco Regis, non aliud est esse talem aliud est haberi pro tali.* I conceive it is high Treason to kill a Lord Deputy, as it is of a Prorex by the Civil Law, and I believe your Lordship never extended your Commission. That your Lordship hath born too strict an hand in your Goverment. Who knows what bridle is best for any horse 'till he knows his conditions? the Asiatic must always be curbed, else all is lost. I know nothing, but whilst I was in Ireland the poor cried never so good a Lord Deputy before, as it was said of Pius V *felix est electio quia gaudent pauperes,* those that durst not speak to your Lordship, *ignorabant clementiam vestram,* and in all cases your Lordship did *patienter audire, perspicuè discernere,* and *recte judicare.*

That your Lordship did exercise Marshal Law *tempore Pacis* : for which some say there are Precedents that is High Treason. *quod non capio.* For, exercising military Discipline being *Bellum repre-sentativum* and done *in forma Guerræ,* the same proceedings may be used as in a real war ; for, *repræsentans debet esse similis et par repræsentato,* the Copy to the Original, as to abuse the Picture of a Nobleman hath been punished in the Star-chamber; and the tender of a Gentlewoman's picture has been decreed to be good in the Court of Wards for the double value of the marriage. And for

Precedents Sr Edward Cooke says, that *duo sunt ad omnes res con-firmandas instrumenta, saltem ratio et authoritas*: in authority we see by other men's eyes, in reason with our own, but *sapientis est proprio lumine videre.* It was formerly Murder to kill a man se defendendo, and some Judgments are only *Lex temporis ad unum intenta, quæ non debent trahi in exemplum*: but in all Treason there must be either some *Inimicitia* against the King, or that which the Civilians call *Crimen Perduellionis, quando quis aliquid directè molitur contra Rempublicam talis est hostis Patriæ*, as was in Dr Story 13 Q. Eliz[æ], which tends to the Destruction of the King, for Majestas est major potestas: can a Lord Deputy committ Treason against the State of Ireland ? If your Lordship did mistake the Law, can that be Treason ? I conceive the Lord Kilmallotkes case did much more approximate the nature of Treason than your Lordship's. Stanley's case, tempore Hen 7, is not *ad rem*, for those Ifs and Ands did imply a doubt of the King's Title, which is *crimen extirpandæ Majestatis.* Nor the Duke of Norfolk's Case any jot parallel, and Brooke in his reading upon 25 Ed. 3, 26, to do Injustice no Treason. That your Lordship should tell a Peer of Ireland, that he should have no other Justice than what was in this breast. These words may admitt a fair construction; for *Rex cen-setur habere omnes leges in scrinio pectoris sui*, and your Lordship being Lieutenant may intend by that to do pure Justice, and St August. lib. de Hær. cap. 86, defends Tertullian, *quod dixerit Deum habere corpus, nam potuit intelligere de corpore concerto, cùm non sit quid inane, sed omnino aliquid, et totus ubique, non autem uti corpus discretum habens partes majores et mincres prout habent corpora nostra, ergo non est blasphemia, quia melius est reddere Deo rationem de Misericordia quam de Crudelitate.* And I know all good men desire your Lordship's Justification, that being more honourable for all, as it is more credit for a Physician that his patient recover than to die under his hands.

That your Lordship should be over-indulgent to the Catholicks more than what Reason of State did require, I do not believe, for I knew your Lordship zealous to suppress Mass-Houses in Dublin, which were converted to Temples, and if it be not too much pre· sumption I would say what Monsieur Provost of Geneve said not long since of your Lordship, *Ce Seigneur quand il estoit icy parmy nous avait une tres genereuse ame, et assurement il estoit en l'estat de Grace*, from which there is no falling. What Acts are Treason our French Advocates discourse copiously; and Popham says that Wolfgangue, Treasurer to Maximilian, spent the Emperor four millions, and yet they could not procced capitally against him. And that case in the 11th Report, fol. 91, that to embezzle Treasure-trouve should be Treason, is such a wasting whereby a Kingdom is actually endamaged, and then *causa causæ est causa causati.*

Your Lordship's Sentence left with Monsieur Cardonie (who rejoices to show the Bed your Lordship lay in) *Qui nimis notus omnibus ignotus moritur sibi,*[a] where there is this likewise, Quamvis *injuria nullos, invidia multos parit inimicos.* 'Tis a high Presumption (unless your Lordship please to give it another name) thus to interrupt your serious affairs, but I hope your Lordship's Goodness, as it doth exceed your greatness, so it will excuse this boldness, and according to the Divine Nature (whose dear servant you are) accept of my affectual desires because *voluntas est mensura actionum, & impotentia excusat legem.* I beseech your Lordship not to wrong my good meaning, to think that I do any way presume to advise your sublime wisdom (though if Solomon should demand an Opinion, he should receive *si non bonum saltem fidele consilium*). This

---

[a] "Among Milton's introductions at Geneva through Diodate or otherwise was one to the family of Camillo Cerdogni or Cardouin, a Neapolitan nobleman, who had been resident in Geneva since 1608 as a Protestant refugee and a teacher in Italian. The family kept an album, in which they liked to collect autographs of strangers passing through the city, and especially of English strangers. Many Englishmen, and some Scotchmen, predecessors of Milton in the usual continental tour, had already left their signatures in this album, and among them no less a man than Wentworth, whose autograph appears in it under date 1612" (Masson, Life of Milton, i. 833, ed. 1881). The album, according to Professor Masson, was once in the possession of Charles Sumner, and is still in America. Strafford's motto is from Seneca. Pope was fond of quoting the same lines (Courthope's Life of Pope, p. 72).

humble presentation of my service, being only what I can testify of it, might any way avail your Lordship, which is a Debt that I owe to Verity. I trust in God, your Lordship will acquit yourself, as did the Lord Wentworth 1 Eliz. for which end my unhallowed prayers shall horarily attend your Honour. The Lord of Life multiply the days of your Lordship's Life, what Period better than Prayer.

> Je suis,
> > Monseigneur,
> > > Vostre tres humble serviteur à jamais,
> > > > JOHN COOKE.

VIII.

[This paper seems to have been written by Strafford himself, for the writer, whilst usually referring to Strafford as " the Earl," twice relapses into the first person and uses the word " me." It is undated, but from the mention of Strafford's letter of May 4, and of the passage of the Attainder Bill through both Houses, it must have been written on or after May 8, on the morning of which day the bill passed the Lords. At nine o'clock on the evening of the 9th the King at last gave way, and promised to pass the bill. The royal assent was actually given, by commissioners, on the morning of the 10th. This paper therefore must have been written on the 8th or 9th, most probably on the former day. Rushworth prints a letter from Strafford to his secretary, Guilford Slingsby (Trial p. 774). Unfortunately this letter also is undated, but it is said by Rushworth to have been written " immediately after the Bill of Attainder did pass both Houses." " Your going to the King," writes Strafford, " is to no purpose, I am lost, my body is theirs, but my soul is God's; there is little trust in man, God may yet (if it please him) deliver me." Then he goes on to refer to some scheme which is his last hope, such as it is. " The person you were last withal at Court sent to move that business we resolved upon, which if rightly handled might perchance do something ; but you know my opinion in all, and what my belief is in all these things."

It is possible that Strafford was referring to some plan for his escape from the Tower. According to Sir William Balfour's deposition of 2 June " the Earl of Strafford sent for him some three or four days before his death, and did strive to perswade him that he might make an escape; and said, for without your connivance I know it cannot be; and if you will consent thereto I will make you to have 20,000 pounds paid you besides a good marriage for your son " (Husband's Exact Collection, p. 233).

It is however more likely that he referred to some such plan as the one described in this paper. Strafford had evidently no great confidence in the success of the plan he refers to. " That business we resolved upon," I take to be the plan that the King should attempt to save Strafford's life by a guarantee that he should never again possess political authority or influence. The person who " sent to move that business " I suppose to be either Bristol or Savile, the prompters of the King's declaration of May 1 in which a similar compromise was offered. This paper resembles that declaration in some of its expressions and statements. Each alike insists on the fact that the King was present all through the trial and was not convinced by what he heard. Each alike insists on the necessity of respecting the King's conscience, and proposes the life-long exclusion of Strafford from power as the sole solution which unites satisfaction for the fears of the people with respect for the conscience of the King. It is the same policy developed and brought up to date, with one new argument in its favour added, viz. the unconstitutional pressure by which the Bill of Attainder had been carried.· In obedience to the suggestion thus conveyed to him, and in order that the " business " might be " rightly handled " Strafford seems to have drawn up these notes, " How the King should behave when the Bill of Attainder against the Earl of Strafford is presented to him."

It was probably sent to the King on the night of the 8th of May. Strafford's letter to Radcliffe, written on the morning of the 9th, is less hopeless than his letter to Slingsby. " Let us see the issue of to-morrow," he says (Whitaker's Life of Sir George Rad-cliffe, p. 224). His only hope must have been in the possible success of the expedient propounded in this paper. " If the King will speak thus much resolutely, it is thought the Earl might yet be saved." No doubt he expected that the King would at least make the attempt, though he can hardly have expected that it would succeed. Hence, what is otherwise unexplained, the sorrow-ful surprise with which Strafford received the news that the King had given his assent to the Bill. The news is said to have reached him through Sir Dudley Carleton, one of the Clerks of the Council. " The Earl, amazed, seriously asked him whether his Majesty had passed the Bill, as not believing, without some astonishment, that the King would have done it. And being again assured that is was passed he arose from his chair, and standing up lift his eyes to Heaven, clapt his hand upon his heart, and said ' Put not your trust in Princes, nor in the sons of men, for in them there is no salvation.' " This story first appears, I believe, in William San-derson's History of the Life and Reign of King Charles, 1658. It is not in the " Brief and Perfect Relation " of Strafford's trial, pub-lished in 1647, nor in L'Estrange's " Reign of King Charles," published in 1654, though L'Estrange is particularly full in his account of the passing of the Attainder Bill.

Whitelocke's version of the story is copied almost verbatim from Sanderson.

A third argument that this paper actually reached the King seems to be afforded by the King's letter to the House of Lords on May 11. He asks them to allow him to show mercy " by suffering that unfortunate man to fulfil the natural course of his life in a close imprisonment: yet so that if ever he make the least offer to escape, or offer directly or indirectly to meddle in any sort of public business, especially with me, by either message or letter, it shall cost him his life without further process " (Lords' Journals, iv., 245). Strafford's paper had suggested " A Bill to disenable me from all publick employments, or giving any counsel directly or indirectly, and if the Earl should offer any such thing to make it high treason, and he to suffer accordingly."]

How the King should behave when the Bill of Attainder against the Earl of Strafforde is presented to him for the Royal Assent.

After the title of the Bill of Attainder read, first his Majesty to cause the Earl's letter of the fourth of May to be read. Then may his Majesty speak something to this purpose: That although here are the votes of both Houses, and the consent of the Party concerned for the passing of this Bill, yet his Majesty may not forbear to declare, that he hath found himself exceedingly perplexed in his thoughts, whether or no to give the Royal Assent to the Bill, wherein every man ought to be so charitable as to believe according as Truth is; that he doth and will verily preferr the Peace of his own Conscience above all other respects whatsoever; that his Majesty had been throwout at the hearing of the cause, and now in the conclusion must have the Liberty allowed him to direct his actions uprightly according to what he finds in his own heart. That he understands this Bill endured a great Debate in the Commons House, and finally a considerable Party gave their negative votes to the Bill, and amongst them most of the ablest and best learned Lawyers of the House. That likewise there were in the Upper House a very considerable Party of the Lords, which also voted against the Passing of the Bill. Which difference of opinions leaves a greater Latitude in his Majesty, with the same freedom to discharge his conscience as others in either House have done, and that more especially in regard it is immediately the King that owes an account to God for the Life of the very meanest of his subjects. Besides there are other two considerations which weigh very much with his Majesty, and which in his opinion set a great Prejudice upon this Bill.

The first that the names of such as voted against the Bill in the Lower House were in an infamous manner posted up and down in several places of the town, to affright and take from men the free delivery of their own opinions, which to endeavour is in itself the greatest Breach of Parliament Privilege, and the most dangerous subverting of Fundamental Laws that can be, thus endeavouring to corrupt the Fountains whence we receive and where all Laws are preserved.

The second, that to the great scandal and offence of the Justice of the Land, the Lords have been in a tumultuary way pressed upon, sundry of them very uncivilly treated both in words and actions, others by those means absenting themselves to avoid the Danger, and others as may be thought less at Liberty to give their votes than otherwise they might have been.

That he must profess, as in the Presence of God, he in his conscience holds the Earl of Strafforde free from any act or intention of Treason at all, and for those words charged and spoken in his Majesty's presence, he also avows them truly to have been spoken as the Earl hath set them forth in his answer and not otherwise. And as for the bringing the Irish Army over to reduce this Kingdom, there was never any such thing spoken in his presence, or ever in the thought of him, or any of that Committee to his knowledge, that any part of that Army should have come on English ground. Hereupon to tell them absolutely he dare not become guilty of shedding bloud by pressing the Bill, but desire them to accept of a Bill to disenable *me* from all publick employment, or giving any counsell directly or indirectly, and if the Earl should offer any such thing, to make it High Treason, and he to suffer for it accordingly, which he will faithfully promise to observe, and so no possibility left, that the Earl, if he had a mind to do it, could procure ill to any body.

Or else that his Majesty would pass the Bill conditionally, that the Houses would consent that his Majesty might at after follow the guide of his own conscience, to pardon the Earl his Life.

That thus every man's Conscience and Fears might be provided for, and his Majesty receive from the two Houses a great argument of their Love towards him, without danger to any body, and in some degree enjoy the Quietness and Repose of his own Conscience by their means. If neither of these could be obtained at his earnest intreaty, that so the publick Peace might more speedily be settled to the contentment both of King and People, wherein he would be wholly counselled by them, he must declare absolutely, that for no respect or fear in the world would he be constrained either actively or passively to take away the Life of a man, where his Conscience was fully informed, He was not guilty of the Crime wherewith he was charged.   .   .

And yet, if the King will speak thus much resolutely, and move the Lords one by one, as also Mr. Solicitor, Pym, and some of the Principal Lower House men, and in the mean time strictly to command Newport[a] to have *me* and this place in safe custody upon the peril of his Life, it is thought the Earl might yet be saved.

---

[a] The Constable of the Tower.

)

www.ingramcontent.com/pod-product-compliance
Lightning Source LLC
Chambersburg PA
CBHW021451090426
42739CB00009B/1708